HEALTHY CHILDREN OF DIVORCE IN 10 SIMPLE STEPS:

Minimize the Effects of Divorce on Your Children

SHANNON RIOS PAULSEN, MS LMFT

LifeThreads Books
Evergreen, CO 80439
www.healthychildrenofdivorce.com
ISBN: 978-0-9916361-0-5

DEDICATION

To Emma Emaya, my beautiful, abundant daughter and light of my life.

To all the children of divorce, may your lights shine brighter.

To all children, may your dreams come true.

CONTENTS

PREFACE
MY STORY

Growing up as a child of high conflict and divorce, I knew there had to be a better way. The hurt and pain I personally experienced and saw in other children, was not an emotionally healthy path. So, I became the voice for the children—a voice I never had as a child.

I became a licensed marriage and family therapist and devoted part of my career to serving children and families of divorce.

This book was written, from my heart, to support you and your children on this journey. Your commitment to your children will make a huge difference in their ability to adjust to the challenge of divorce and to emerge emotionally healthy and happy. I wish you and your children the very best.

—Shannon Rios Paulsen, MS LMFT
www.healthychildrenofdivorce.com
www.inlovewithme.com
www.rioscoaching.com
www.manifestingbaby.com

INTRODUCTION
WHY READ AND COMPLETE THIS WORKBOOK?

This 10-step workbook is designed to help you be the best parent possible for your child before, during, and after a divorce/separation. If you want to take proactive steps to protect your children, you are in the right place. My goal is to teach you what I have learned working as a licensed marriage and family therapist with thousands of families of divorce and conflict over the past twelve years so you can successfully parent your children through this transition.

My experience as a child of divorce led me to this work. I began as a children's therapist, but quickly realized I also wanted to work directly with parents because ultimately, you hold the key to your child's happiness and success. Thus, I began teaching *Co-parenting after Divorce* and have taught this course to thousands of parents.

I also wrote the best-selling book *The 7 Fatal Mistakes Divorced and Separated Parents Make: Strategies for Raising Healthy Children of Divorce and Conflict*. Now, I have created this simple, easy-to-follow workbook that includes the most crucial information divorcing parents must know. Reading and following the steps in this book may be one of the most important gifts you ever give your children. I do this work from my heart for one reason – to ensure we raise the healthiest and happiest children. They deserve this.

If you take all of the steps outlined in this workbook seriously and implement the strategies, you will successfully raise healthy children of divorce.

It will take <u>choice</u> and <u>commitment</u>.

How This Book Will Help Your Children

1. **Your actions as a parent and co-parent = your child's emotional and physical health.** Judith Wallerstein found in her long-term research that "the quality of the child's relationship with each parent and the relationship between parents are key factors in the child's emotional and social adjustment after divorce."

2. **You are now connected to your co-parent for life.** Because you made a choice to have a child, you and this person are now connected for life. Many different occasions will

bring the two of you back together again and again for some of the most important events of your child's life (birthdays, holidays, first day of preschool, first day of kindergarten, kindergarten graduation, plays and concerts, sporting events, high school and other post-secondary graduations, possibly a wedding and then… yes, the birth of your grandkids). You will want to be certain that your child can enjoy these events without worrying and stressing about you and your co-parent's behavior.

3. **Children of divorce have significantly more issues than children from non-divorced homes.** Children from divorced homes have more illnesses, medical problems, and physician visits than children from non-divorced families. They are also three times more likely to receive psychological treatment. Research also shows that twenty-five percent (25%) of children from divorced families have serious social, emotional, and psychological problems, compared to ten percent (10%) of children from non-divorced families. I firmly believe that if you follow the steps outlined in this workbook, you can significantly reduce these issues for your children.

4. **Healing yourself is the key.** If you take time to heal your own pain over the ending of your relationship, you will be able to be the best parent possible for your child. If you neglect to heal yourself, you will most likely be stuck in anger or depression and your child can get stuck there with you. Healing yourself is a choice. To not choose the healing path puts your child's emotional and physical health at risk.

5. **Your child is counting on you.** It is your job (that you accepted when you chose to be a parent) to provide the best foundation and support possible for him or her to grow into a successful adult. This is the most important job you will ever have.

6. **A good relationship with your co-parent = a good outcome for your kids.** One study reported that when parents related to each other in a healthy manner after divorce and conflict was low, their children felt that in the long run, they were better off or were not affected by their parents' divorce. This conclusion was based on a study of 173 adults who experienced divorce as children.

7. **You love your child.** You want to ensure his or her future success. The choices you make now will impact your children for the rest of their lives. Your choices will influence your child's self-esteem, confidence, relationships, and overall success in life. We now know if you follow the steps in this book, you will be taking the necessary steps to protect your child from the negative effects of divorce.

For Your Child: This Is an Emergency

I ask you now from my heart to see this divorce or co-parenting situation as an emergency for your child. Your child's health and happiness are on the line.

The analogy of this situation being an "emergency" for your child came from my own childhood. You see, at one point, I was hit by a car as I was riding my bike. It was very serious. My parents traveled together to see me, they stood together at my bedside, and were able to put all their conflict aside. This was a small miracle for them at that point. Thankfully, when my life was at stake, in an emergency situation, they put me first.

I ask you now to think of what you are going through in the same way. I ask you to consider the next few years as an emergency. Your child's health and happiness truly are in danger if you continue negative behaviors around the divorce situation—so this is a true emergency. Do your best to effectively work with your co-parent and do the work to heal yourself—this will ensure your child's optimal health. In life, we call the emergency number when we need help or are in danger. Imagine dialing the emergency number when you think about doing harmful behaviors during this divorce. I ask you to dial the emergency number in your mind, listen to the operator, who will be me, and keep your kids safe. You will be so glad you did.

The Most Important Job in the World

Yes, you did it! You achieved the highest status of all, that of PARENT. This is something to be so grateful for. Not every person gets this privilege.

When you signed up to be a parent, you made a choice to guide your children through life and provide them love, nurturing, and skills to be a successful person.

Now, you are taking on the new role of parenting your child through your divorce. The choices you make now will impact your children for the rest of their lives. Your choices will impact their self-esteem, confidence, relationships, and overall success in life. You and your co-parent chose to have a child and now your child needs both of you to respect each other so he/she can have a calm and peace-filled life. If you complete this workbook and apply it to your life, your children will thank you. Either they will personally tell you or you will see it for yourself as they thrive and grow into healthy and successful adults.

Your children are counting on you. They want to be able to create their most amazing life and they need your full love, attention, and support to do this.

Ask yourself the six-million-dollar question: *Is your child's future worth taking a few hours to read and then apply what you learn in this workbook?*

If your answer to this question is yes, I congratulate you from my heart for taking this important first step to protect and love your children. Let's get started!

Throughout this book, you will see icons to indicate some important information, exercises, emergency topics or healthy/unhealthy parenting examples. They will be indicated by the following icons:

 Information

The Information sections will give you facts and data relating to parenting

 Exercises

The Exercises sections will be hands on learning that you can do to really understand the concepts presented in this book and apply them to yourself and your children.

 Emergency Parenting Tips

Parent Tip sections feature topics that are especially critical to the health and well-being of your children. Pay extra attention to the Emergency Parenting Tip boxes! These represent some of the most important tips to becoming a good co-parent.

  Healthy and Unhealthy Parent Examples

These are all stories taken from true situations I have experienced working as a kids therapist and divorce and parenting class facilitator over the last fourteen years. They are to help you understand what your kids are going through and how best to help them be happy and healthy through the divorce process.

STEP #1
FOCUS ON THE FUTURE

 Focus on What You Can Control

You may feel you do not have a lot of control as you move through the divorce process. You may be overwhelmed initially by the changes in routines, roles and responsibility. You may not know how you will support two homes financially, what days of the week you will be seeing your children, where you will live, and sometimes even when you will see the children next. All of these scenarios may create anxiety and fear for parents going through divorce.

The goal is to move from the fear of what you can't control to embracing what you CAN control. When we think about the future, we actually feel calmer inside; it activates the rational part of our brain.

What You Can Control—Focus Forward on the Most Important Things

No matter what is currently happening in your family, you have a lot of control over what is going to happen in your future. The questions below are areas you have direct control over as the next days, weeks, and years unfold. Focus on these.

Answer the following three questions (please be sure to write out your responses in the space provided):

1. What do you want for your children's future?
Write your wishes and then envision or imagine this happening for your children.

_____

_____

_____

2. What do you want your future relationship with your children to be like?
Write these hopes down and then envision or imagine what this looks like in your mind.

---

3. How do you want your children to adjust to this divorce or transition in your family?
Write this down and see this happening in your mind.

📖 Creating Your New Life with Your Children: Focus on Three Words

What three words describe the new family you want to create with your children? Some good suggestions include: Loving, Peaceful, Happy, Joy, Communicate, Breathe, Hugs, Connection, Honesty, or Fun. Choose three words now and write them here. You may want to ask your children to help you choose the family words. Once you have chosen each word, then explain how you will demonstrate that word in your family. *Example: Loving—we will hug each other daily. We will say we love each other every day, when my kids are with me.*

1.

2.

3.

I ask you to think about these words often and check-in to see if you are building your desired family environment. These words will help keep you honest. How will you keep these values alive? Ideas include: post them on a door or the refrigerator; hold a family meeting each week to discuss how everyone is doing honoring the family's values; discuss them each night with your kids; or set a reminder on your phone.

 ## Healthy Parent: Move Forward So Your Children Can Move Forward

One mother came to me after her children's father decided out of nowhere he wanted a divorce. She felt very wronged, hurt, and disempowered. Her children were mad at their father for *"doing this"* to their mother. She asked what she could do to help her children. I told her, *"You can help yourself. You are a strong individual. Stop blaming their father and your children will too. Move forward with your life and your kids can move forward, too. Show your kids you are strong."* She did this and her life moved forward and so did her children's. In time, they were also able to forgive their dad and have a healthy relationship with him.

When you hold anger at your co-parent, you hold your children back from living the life they are here to live. Let it go; it serves no purpose.

Ask Yourself: What positive step do I need to take to move forward in my life?

STEP #2
ESTABLISH HEALTHY COMMUNICATION

 Communication

Continued conflict between parents is very damaging to your children. It can impact the following:

- Self-esteem
- At-risk behaviors
- School performance
- Peer relationships
- Physical health

Conflict on the outside between parents creates conflict on the inside for your children. This conflict inside can create chronic stress, anxiety, and/or health issues for your children.

 Dig Deep—Assess Conflict Level before Separation/Divorce, Currently, and in the Future

It is important to think about the level of conflict you truly want with your co-parent long-term.

Assess your conflict level on a scale of 1–10 at the following points in time (before, current and future) by circling the number on the scale below (1 = very low or no conflict; 10 = very high or always in conflict).

Circle the number that represents the level of conflict with your spouse/partner *before* the divorce/separation occurred:

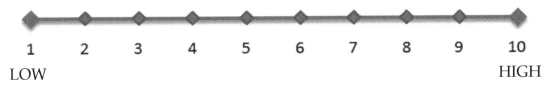

Circle the number that represents the *current* level of conflict with your spouse/partner.

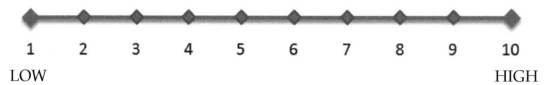

| 1 | 2 | 3 | 4 | 5 | 6 | 7 | 8 | 9 | 10 |
| LOW | | | | | | | | | HIGH |

Circle the number that represents the desired *future* level of conflict (remember the divorce is your opportunity to do things differently if they were not optimal in the past):

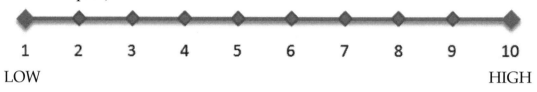

| 1 | 2 | 3 | 4 | 5 | 6 | 7 | 8 | 9 | 10 |
| LOW | | | | | | | | | HIGH |

✚ Emergency Parenting Tip: Conflict

Every time you feel the urge to fight or have a negative reaction toward your co-parent, imagine your child in an emergency room. Know that you hold the key to their health and well-being. Your child needs your love, support and peace.

ASK YOURSELF: Is fighting with my co-parent really worth damaging my child's emotional and physical health?

 ## Unhealthy Parenting: Teaching Your Child by Telling Them Your Co-Parent is Crazy

Ben was twelve-years old. His mother had been posting articles on Facebook about narcissism and talking with Ben about this behavior of his father's. When her co-parent brought this up in a joint parent coaching session, she told me she had been sharing these with Ben to "help him understand how to deal with his father." This child was confused and felt he was crazy because his dad was crazy. His mom telling him negative things about his dad was increasing Ben's anxiety and he did not want to spend time with his dad.

Shannon's Coaching: If a parent has concerns about the other parent's behaviors, it is best to teach your child skills to deal with that behavior without talking about your co-parent directly.

For example, if you believe your co-parent is a chronic liar, you want to teach your child the value of telling the truth and provide them with positive examples of telling the truth (as they arise in your lives). You should never teach your child using negative examples of your co-parent. Your child can learn to deal with your co-parent through the positive behaviors/skills you teach them.

Ask Yourself: What behaviors concern you about your co-parent that you know your child will have to deal with? How can you teach your child skills to deal with these behaviors in a positive way without saying anything negative about your co-parent?

Complete the Parent Basher Quiz

It is important to be aware of behaviors that can harm your child. Check the "Yes" box if you have ever done any of the following:

	Yes	No
I sometimes say negative things to my child about their other parent.	❑	❑
I sometimes get frustrated, verbally or non-verbally, in front of my child when my child's other parent does or says something I do not like.	❑	❑
I sometimes say negative things in front of my child about their other parent's new partner.	❑	❑
I talk negatively to my friends and relatives on the phone about my child's other parent when my child is present. (Note: Even if a child is in another room, they have a keen ability to hear your conversation.)	❑	❑
I quiz my child for anything negative that may have happened while they were in their other parent's care.	❑	❑
I try to make my child feel guilty about spending time with their other parent.	❑	❑
I try to manipulate my co-parent's time with our kids.	❑	❑

I say things to my child like, "He never wanted to spend time with you when we were together. I have no idea what has changed all of a sudden."   ❏   ❏

I say negative things to my friends and family about my children's other parent with my children present. Or, I allow my family and friends to say negative things to me about my co-parent when my children are present.   ❏   ❏

 ## These Behaviors Can Be Damaging for Both Your Child and You for Many Reasons:

1. **Children do not separate themselves from their parents.** If you say negative things about your co-parent, your child feels you are also directing the negative feelings toward him or her.

2. **Over time, being a parent basher will backfire on you.** In time, your child will start to resent you for being so negative. At some point, children will base their opinion of your co-parent on their co-parent's actual behaviors, not your words. You will end up looking like the bitter and ridiculous one. Children tire of a negative parent over time. Parents who are negative about their co-parent are sometimes negative parents in general, which is not a healthy environment for your child.

3. **Being a parent basher is a complete waste of time.** Your frustration at your co-parent pulls you away from loving your child. It takes time and energy away from your ability to connect with and love your child. Don't waste this precious energy on your co-parent, save it to spend happy quality time with your child.

Assess the Impact of Conflict

What is the impact of conflict with your co-parent on your own life?

_____

_____

_____

How do you think it affects your children to hear fighting between the two people they love the most?

_____

_____

_____

Why is it important to your child for you to reduce your conflict with your co-parent and increase your positive communication?

_____

_____

_____

 ## Unhealthy Parents: Stuck in a Pattern of Fighting

Kids get so confused by your fighting with your co-parent even after the divorce. I was working with an eight-year-old girl named Marcy and when I asked her if she felt this was her fault she said to me, "Well, they fight a lot about me and so I think this is my fault."

This child's parents fought a lot after the divorce. This caused Marcy to have stress inside. She actually thought that because her parents were fighting about her (they were fighting over parenting time and any other issue to do with her) that this was her fault. She had been waking up at night and throwing up. Her older sister became extremely concerned and thought Marcy may be really sick. Her sister and father took Marcy to the doctor and the doctor asked, "Has she been under a lot of stress lately?" She sure had. The throwing up was Marcy literally purging the stress she took in from all her parents fighting. They were putting her in the middle and not moving forward with their lives in a healthy way.

Shannon's Coaching: Do your best to not fight with your co-parent around your children—in front of them, in another room, or on the phone where they could hear you. This cycle of fighting must be disrupted for the sake of your children's stress and your stress. If you cannot do this on your own, seek professional support.

Ask Yourself: Am I stuck in a pattern of fighting with my co-parent? What do I know I need to do to change it?

✚ Emergency Parenting Tip: Refocus Your Energy

Take one day and assess the percentage of time you spend being negative versus the percentage of time you spend being positive. Take the negative energy you may have been wasting on your co-parent in the past and redirect this energy to loving and spending quality time with your child. Every time you want to be frustrated with your co-parent, reach out and love your child. You can also do something loving for yourself. Don't focus on your co-parent; this is a waste of your time and energy. Focus on enjoying your children and looking forward to your new future.

 ## Good Qualities of Your Co-Parent (Yes, I Said GOOD)

*All your child wants is for the two people who brought them into this world (or raised them) to respect each other. They want **you to respect** their **mom** for one simple reason: she is their **mom**. They want **you to respect** their **dad** for one simple reason: he is their **dad**.*

It is also positive for you to see your co-parent's good qualities because their good qualities mean, despite how the relationship has changed, you chose someone who has good characteristics. The fact that your co-parent has some good qualities says something positive about you. It also tells your child there is something good about them since they are genetically related to this person or they were raised by and love this person.

It is crucial for your children to hear you say something positive about their other parent. It helps lower their stress and fear.

List Two Good Qualities About Your Co-Parent

This could be: they have a job, they are a good cook, they are patient, or they are organized. Anything you can later say to your child, such as *"I bet you had a great time eating at Dad's this weekend. He is such a good cook."*

1. _____

_____

_____

2. _____

_____

_____

 ## Important Fact: Not All Families Have Conflict

I estimate that about fifty percent (50%) of families that divorce do not experience high conflict before the divorce. If you were a family with low or no conflict, this can pose other challenges for your children. Kids whose parents did not have high conflict before the divorce can be very confused about why their parents are divorcing. These children may have a higher rate of blaming themselves. They also may want to blame the divorce on one of you. Many kids in this scenario have shared with me that during the divorce the conflict between parents is sometimes higher (which makes sense, since you may now be arguing over finances or parenting time, which were not issues before). However, that means these kids are now dealing with both the divorce and a higher degree of conflict. Kids report this is not fun (and quite difficult) for them.

If you had lower conflict before the divorce, you have a bigger job now to ensure that divorce-related conflict (i.e., parenting time and financials) does not spiral out of control. Your goal is to get your conflict back to the level of where it was prior to the divorce as quickly as possible.

Strategies for Effective and Healthy Communication

Strategy#1: Choose to Take the High Road

If there is one concept I hope will stay with you after reading this book, this one is close to the top of my list. In the co-parenting class I teach, parents say, *"I am the one who always buys notebooks for my child."* What I say is, *"If you are not able to civilly communicate about this, then take the high road. If notebooks (or pants, shoes, or diapers) are worth a huge argument, then you are not willing to put your child's needs first."*

This anger is not about the notebook. The notebook represents your old unresolved issues and anger at this person. Let the old anger go. Don't sweat the small stuff. Let the small stuff go. It is just not worth compromising your child's emotional well-being.

Action:
With your palm open and facing down, lift your arm as if you are pushing up toward the sky and say to yourself, "I now choose to take the high road." This is the adult option. Please make the effort to actually, physically do this. Doing this exercise now will help you do it when co-parenting issues arise; it is important to take the high road whenever possible. It may be a skill you need to develop and use often.

Strategy #2: Pick Your Battles

A previous manager of mine said to me, "Shannon, I have learned to pick my battles." She was indicating there were things she chose to ignore because it would entail a huge uphill climb. Make sure the issues you choose to bring to your co-parent's attention are really worth the amount of effort you may extend in arguing with them.

Action:
Always assess the cost/benefit ratio of your actions. Make sure the cost of bringing the issue up will reap a big enough benefit.

Strategy #3: Don't Act in Anger

Acting in anger NEVER accomplishes anything positive. We all know this, but it can be so hard to remember in the moment. Remember, no one ever actually makes us angry; it is always a choice we make. If you feel frustrated by your co-parent, always give yourself some time to calm down so you can think clearly.

Action:

Vow never to speak to your co-parent when you are angry. Ask yourself why this situation is so frustrating for you. What are you telling yourself about this situation that makes it so frustrating? Take your own time-out if you are feeling angry. Do something healthy to calm down. The good news is that you always have choices.

Action:

Use the following acronym the next time you want to say something in frustration to your co-parent: WAIT—which stands for Why Am I Talking? This will help you to stop and assess if what you are planning to say or are saying will create a healthy co-parenting relationship.

Strategy #4: Kill 'Em with Kindness:

Yes, it is true, being extra nice works. It is so hard to be rude to someone when they are nice to us. Another way to say this is, "Fake it 'til you make it." It is proven that this simple strategy lowers high conflict over time.

Action:

Be overly nice to your co-parent in your next interaction with them. See how it goes.

Strategy #5: Be Curious:

Remember Curious George? Think of him now as your best friend for a while. This friend sits on your shoulder and says, "Be curious." Don't blame or accuse, just ask dumb/curious questions about any issue that comes up between you and your co-parent.

Action:

Be curious the next time your co-parent does something ridiculous. This really diffuses a lot of defensiveness. This works with kids and co-workers, too.

Strategy #6: Create a Structure to Remember the Strategies

Remembering to use the strategies will be the key to your success. What structure will you use to make sure you remember to act differently the next time you are interacting with your co-parent?

Action:
Set your co-parent's photo on your phone to something like Curious George, Buddha, your favorite comedian, or whatever image works for you in order to remember curiousness, kindness, or laughter. This will help reduce possible conflict. The photo will pop up when they call you and remind you to keep the peace and remember your child. Buy a Curious George toy, print out a picture of Curious George or any other animal or put a note on your computer. To remind you of the love for your child when you feel frustrated wear a special bracelet/necklace, etc..

 ## The Ultimate Strategy: See Your Co-Parent as Your New Business Partner

This other person is now your partner in the most important business of your life. You are co-CEOs, raising your children to be healthy and happy. It is very important to see your co-parent this way. This is a job you don't get to quit. Raising your kids is the biggest product launch of your life and they are counting on you to be a good business partner with their other parent.

Action:
Each time you interact with your co-parent, pretend you are at an important business meeting and your boss is there watching your interactions and your strategy.

Action:
Focus strategically on the next goal for your children that you can both agree on (i.e. getting them through the next grade level, helping them find what they will do after high school, getting them potty trained).

 ## Unhealthy Parenting: Putting Your Child in the Middle of Adult Issues

Jenny was thirteen years old. Her parents had recently divorced. Jenny's mother had been coming to her father's house to visit Jenny (per her request due to her work schedule). However, Mom would always find something to be angry about when she was at Dad's house. She became especially angry once Dad began dating someone new and this new person could not be at Dad's house when Mom was there. When Jenny's dad finally set boundaries and told Mom to have her visits at her own home going forward, Mom became very angry and went to Jenny to ask if she wanted her mom at her dad's house. This was so confusing and upsetting for Jenny. This type of behavior was one example of mom becoming angry at dad and putting Jenny in the middle of their arguments. Jenny became a stressed and anxious kid, not knowing what to say to her mother. She said to her father, "This is never going to get better because she is mentally unstable." Because of her mother's reactions, Jenny was very introverted, stressed, and anxious.

Shannon's Coaching: Putting your child in the middle of your anger and arguments is very challenging for children to understand. Asking your child their opinion on issues you and your co-parent do not agree on is not okay. In this situation, I was working with Dad and strongly recommended he get his daughter in for counseling. This is the best thing to do if your co-parent is putting your child in the middle. Jenny was able to share her feelings with her mom and dad through the help of a counselor.

Ask Yourself: Am I putting my child in the middle of my issues with my co-parent? Is my co-parent doing this? Do we need to seek support?

 ## Prepare Your Family Mission Statement

Family Mission Statement

WE ARE (insert name of child or children) _____ INC.

Business Purpose: Our business is to raise healthy and happy kids of divorce and (insert what is true for you) _____

_____

We commit to doing the following as co-parents to help lower conflict and increase positive communication:

_____

_____

_____

✚ Emergency Parenting Tip:
Laughter is the Best Medicine

Just begin to laugh at the things your co-parent does. Is it really worth it to get upset? We know laughter actually is healing for us. Let your co-parent contribute to your health versus take away your health. Remember the last frustrating thing they did and laugh about it right now.

STEP #3
YOUR CHILD'S BIRTHRIGHT: ALLOWING YOUR CHILD TO LOVE BOTH OF YOU

I can guarantee you one thing; your child did not choose this divorce. They should not be forced to choose between their parents because this puts your children in a very stressful situation. They also should never have to hide their love of one parent from the other parent. This creates a very unhealthy pattern in your child. It tells them they can't love someone very important to them and thus, truly, they can't love a part of themselves. Children cannot develop healthy self-esteem (i.e. self-love) if they are told both or one of their parents is bad. Because to them, it means they are bad. Being told they should not love a parent also tells them they don't deserve to be happy. Don't let your anger or jealousy with your co-parent let you believe that your child should not love your co-parent. These two things should have nothing to do with each other. Your child gets to love both of their parents. In fact, you should encourage this. If you don't allow your child to love their other parent, there is but one word for you—selfish. *Selfish parents lead to sad and confused children.* We know children do better when they have two parents supporting them in life.

Your Co-Parent Is Not Your Ex-Partner

It is really important to understand that your co-parent is different from your ex-partner. If you believe your ex-partner had some bad behaviors toward you, it is time now to put those in the past and allow your ex-partner to assume his or her new identity as your co-parent. The truth is that it takes different skills to be a parent versus a romantic partner. Some people may not be good at romantic partnerships, but that does not necessarily make them bad parents. I had one mother who said her child's father must be bad because he was terrible to her (she said he cheated). However, when I assessed his skills, the father was actually a very good parent to his daughter.

📖 Answer the Following Questions:

1. Could your negative thoughts and feelings about your co-parent (regarding your romantic relationship with them) be impacting your ability to see your co-parent as a good parent for your child? ☐ Yes ☐ No. Why?

_____

_____

_____

2. Can you agree being a romantic partner and being a parent require different skills? The truth is some people can be good parents, but not good romantic partners. Is your co-parent one of these people? ☐ Yes ☐ No. Why?

_____

_____

_____

3. Are you willing to let go of your anger and frustration with this person for not being the best partner for you, so you can see them as the best possible parent for your child? ☐ Yes ☐ No. Why?

_____

_____

_____

4. Can you allow your child to freely love their other parent? ☐ Yes ☐ No. Why is this important?

_____

_____

_____

5. What do you need to do to ensure your child knows it is okay to love their mom/dad?

_____

_____

_____

Now, to complete this exercise, say the statement below aloud:

My experience with my child's other parent as a partner is separate from their ability to effectively parent my child. I choose to let go of my anger and forgive them. I agree to let go of any jealousy I am feeling about my child and their other parent's relationship. I will simply focus on my relationship with my child and be the best parent possible. I choose to see my child's mom/dad as the parent of my child and not as my ex-partner. I choose to create a new and respectful relationship with my child's other parent because my child deserves this.

 ## Ideas for Supporting Your Child's Relationship with Your Co-Parent

1. Choose to separate your own thoughts, emotions, and experiences with your ex-partner from your co-parent's parental role.

2. Give your child the greatest gift of all—the ability to freely love their other parent.

3. Choose to allow your child to see their parent (as long as it is safe).

4. If your co-parent asks you to take care of your child during their parenting time, do not worry about what your co-parent is doing, just be grateful for the extra time with your child.

5. Never withhold your child's parenting time with your co-parent because your co-parent has not paid their child support. This is literally holding your child hostage.

6. Do something kind for your child's other parent. Help your child get a birthday card or present for them. This may be hard, but do it anyway.

✚ Emergency Parenting Tip:
Allow Your Child to Love Both Parents

Envision your child standing between you and your co-parent. They are holding both of your hands. They are so happy inside that the two people who chose to bring them into this world can respect each other and be kind to one another, even through a divorce. Their heart is happy and their self-love grows. This is the greatest gift you can give your child of divorce.

 ## Healthy Parenting: Allowing Your Child to be a Child

Jennifer was twelve when her parents divorced. Her parents made an agreement never to put their child in the middle of adult issues. They worked with a mediator to ensure they both compromised to make the best decisions for their daughter. Each of them agreed to receive their own counseling to help them deal with their anger and hurt at the other parent. They encouraged Jennifer to go out and have fun with her friends and be a kid. Jennifer did not like the divorce, but inside she always felt loved. She was a secure and happy child even though her parents were divorced. She went on to have a healthy relationship and marriage.

Ask Yourself: What can I do to allow my child to be a child right now?

STEP #4
LETTING GO: MOVING ON WITH YOUR LIFE

 Grieve this Loss and Choose to Let Go

Divorce is like a death and you will grieve this loss. There are five steps to the grief process: denial, anger, bargaining, fear/depression, and acceptance. This is not a linear process. One day you may feel sad, one day happy and accepting, the next day, angry. This is normal. The usual amount of time it takes to go through all the stages of grief is twelve to eighteen months. Your children will also go through the grief process and feel these emotions. It is healthy to process emotions. It is only unhealthy **if** you get stuck in any of these steps. If you are stuck in anger, sadness or depression over the ending of this relationship, you are not letting go of this relationship. If you are stuck somewhere in the grief cycle, it creates a situation where you and your child can't move on.

If you are not letting go, neither can your child. If you are stuck in anger or sadness, your child will get stuck there, too. They can only be as healthy as you are. Choose to let go and live a healthy life loving your children instead of focusing on a door that has closed. If you continue to look backward at your co-parent, you cannot be present for your child.

The following diagram is the grief cycle. It is important to assess where you are in the cycle of grief. This assessment will allow you to decide what steps you may need to take to heal so you and your children can move forward.

📖 Understand the Grief Cycle

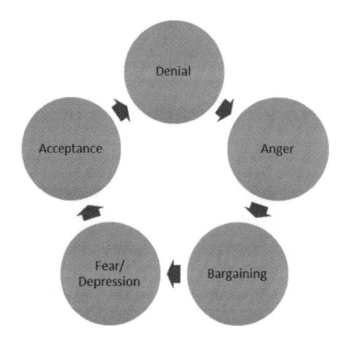

Grief cycle model from Elisabeth Kubler-Ross, *On Death and Dying*, 1969

1. Which of these emotions have you felt?

_____

_____

_____

2. Do you feel like you are stuck in any of these emotions?

_____

_____

_____

3. Is being stuck in one of these emotions impacting your ability to parent your child?

_____

_____

_____

4. Can you make a choice now to move out of this place? What is one step you can take to move yourself forward?

_____

_____

_____

5. If the answer to the previous question is "no," what will you do to seek support?

_____

_____

_____

6. What can you do to help your child process their emotions?

_____

_____

_____

STEP #5
BE RESPONSIBLE: WE ALL CREATE OUR LIFE

 I am going to be honest here. Victims do not make good parents. Victims blame everyone else for how their life looks. If I have learned one thing during my lifetime, it is that my life looks the way it does due to actions I have taken.

Parents who operate as victims create an unhealthy environment for their children filled with stress. They also do not teach children to be responsible. It is time now to make a choice; a choice to not blame anyone else.

Some people tell me all the bad things their co-parent did and I can agree, some of those things are bad. However, I need to make you aware of something. *You chose this person at one point and then you chose to have a child with them.* If you are responsible for nothing else, you must be responsible for this. It is crucial because once you are aware of and responsible for your choices, you can then make a different choice for a healthier future. To be clear, there is absolutely no judgment here, I know we all do our best in choosing partners. I believe we do the best we can with the skills we have at the time.

Unfortunately, humans have an amazing tendency to repeat past relationship choices. If your co-parent was unhealthy for you (i.e. domestic violence, alcoholism), once again choosing someone just like your co-parent would not be healthy for your children. Realizing we were responsible for choosing our co-parent is so important. It gives us data so we can make a healthier future choice.

 ## The Unhealthy Parent: The Victim

Tim's mother would not move forward after her divorce. She continued to blame his father for the end of their marriage. Every chance she got she told him his father was a bad man because he did not want to take them back. She also shared all the sordid details of what she believed Tim's father did to her in the past and in the present. Tim experienced so much stress inside because he felt responsible for his mother and her feelings. He felt like making his mother happy was his responsibility. He also was really confused because he loved his dad. He also loved his mom. Tim had a hard time in school and making friends because he was literally stuck in his mother's pain. He wondered if he was a bad kid because he had a bad dad. He was confused. Tim went on to marry a woman who blamed him for everything and fulfilled his feeling/story that he was a bad person.

Shannon's Coaching: When you stay stuck so do your children. When you tell your children their other parent is bad, you are hurting your child. You are telling them they are bad which over time erodes their self-esteem. The best thing to do is NOT focus your energy on your co-parent. Use your energy to make a plan to get healthy and commit to moving forward. One girl said, "When my mom did better, I did better." They feel so much better when you begin to move forward toward a positive outcome in your life. Your behavior (positive or negative) is continuously a model to your children and it will impact how they live their lives.

Ask Yourself: What am I teaching my children through my current behaviors that they are witnessing? What do I want to teach my children?

Assess Your Ability to Be Responsible and Move Forward

Answer **Yes** or **No** to each question:

	Yes	**No**
• When explaining why you divorced or separated, do you say your child's other parent was the main reason?	☐	☐
• Do you tell the other person they are to blame?	☐	☐
• Do you feel anger on a daily basis toward your child's other parent?	☐	☐
• Do you ever feel it would be best to get back together even though the other person does not want that or has moved on?	☐	☐
• Have you tried to get the other person to reconcile months after separating (and it did not work and you still want to be with this person)?	☐	☐
• Have you been separated for over a year and the divorce is still not final due to unresolved issues (money, house, etc.)?	☐	☐

Ask yourself the following questions to get clarity:

1. What is my payoff for continuing to blame my ex-partner and being stuck in this relationship's pain/anger? Whenever we are stuck somewhere, there is some type of payoff. This may be that you feel you have to control the situation; that you may feel safer not moving forward, change is scary; or that you don't deserve better, etc.

_____

_____

_____

2. Can I begin to see that all relationships take two people to exist and I am responsible for choosing this person? Can I see I am at least partially responsible for the relationship not working? Can I accept there is no blame, only responsibility?

_____

_____

_____

3. What action can I take to let my anger/pain go? What do I need to do to be complete with this relationship/stress/anger/pain/sadness?

_____

_____

_____

 ## A Responsible Parent Forgives

One very special girl came into my office for my initial typical three counseling sessions. Her mom was being pro-active and wanted to ensure the health of her children. Her parents had gone through a challenging divorce, but had been doing better in the last few months. I asked her what she thought about the divorce.

She told me, *"Now that this divorce is over, I think my parents should sit down and apologize to each other." —Girl, age 5*

Kids are very wise. Please take the wisdom of this beautiful child and apologize to those to whom you know you need to apologize. Let it go and start a new life of love and peace. You deserve this and your children deserve this.

To respect your co-parent you must forgive them for what they did. Forgiveness is not forgetting; it is simply choosing to move forward in your life. Forgiveness is for you and your child. It allows you to get unstuck from this past relationship. Forgiveness allows your child to move forward in his or her life, as well.

Always remember, carrying resentment is like taking poison
and expecting the other person to die.

AND

"Forgive them, for they know not what they do." —Lk 23:34:

📖 Practice Forgiveness

1. Are you willing to teach your child forgiveness by showing forgiveness to their other parent? Remember, forgiveness is really not about your co-parent, it is for you, so you can move forward as a parent and a person. ☐ Yes ☐ No. Why?

_____

_____

_____

2. Make a list of all the things you are angry at your ex-partner for. If it is a long list that is fine. You may want to do this exercise on a separate sheet of paper so you can easily dispose of it when you are done.

_____

_____

_____

3. At the very bottom of the above list write, "I choose to forgive my co-parent for these things so I can see them as the best possible parent for my child."

4. You may want to tear up this sheet, burn it, or bury it, symbolizing letting go of these hurts. Let it out, be angry if you want. Releasing emotions in healthy ways can be healing for us.

5. Have you forgiven yourself so you can move forward? Why or why not?

_____

_____

_____

 ## Teach Your Child Respect by Respecting Your Co-Parent

I know this can seem like the hardest one. Yet, it is crucial. Parents, do you want your child to respect you? I think most will answer with a resounding, "Yes." Then why would you not respect (in front of them) the other person who brought them into this world? This is all your children want, for you to respect their other parent for this plain and simple reason—this is their parent. They love this person and are a part of this person. If you are not respecting this other person your child is half of, it is as if you are not respecting your child. Please choose to give your child this respect of respecting your co-parent. You will teach them to respect others and themselves.

This person is a part of your child, so when you respect them, you are respecting your child.

 ## Respect Your Co-Parent

What is one thing you can do to respect your co-parent to your children? (e.g. saying something positive about your co-parent, not saying negative things about your co-parent, being kind to them during drop-offs, etc.)

_____

_____

_____

STEP #6
DATING: PROCEED WITH CAUTION.
YOUR CHILDREN ARE AT RISK!

After years of experience as a kids' therapist, I have witnessed and determined that after conflict, dating is the next biggest risk factor for your children. Dating is not exciting for your children. I have had children say to me, "I feel like they are trying to replace my mom/dad." Your children do not want another mom or dad right now. They want to process this divorce and spend healthy, quality time with you for at least the first year. Take dating slow and easy, you have a posse behind you now (your kids). Another person adds an extra dynamic that your children have to deal with. They are dealing with enough right now.

The Red Flags are Bigger Now

When you begin to date, your kids are counting on you to do so wisely. You have to be sure this is a good person for you first and then assess if they are also good for your children. The truth is they can be good for you and not your kids (jealous of your kids, different parenting style, don't really like kids, etc.). I always say "the red flags are bigger now". When you were single without kids, dating was different. You are now a parent whose number one job is to protect your children and keep them safe. You must pay close attention to the behaviors of the person you are dating. If you see anything that you do not feel is healthy, you need to take more time to assess this person before introducing them to your children (or simply quickly end the relationship) so your kids are not put through another unhealthy relationship or divorce.

The other important point to understand is that your children may grow attached to this person. If you break up with your partner, your children will suffer another loss. This can be hard for them and it can be another opportunity for them to blame themselves. This is important to understand, so you can communicate with your children about their feelings if you do end a future relationship.

Blending Two Families

Blending families and taking on other people's children (if you marry someone who already has children as well) is much harder than most people could ever imagine. I have seen so many failed blended families. Parents seem to think a new partner can easily accept their existing children. This is not the reality in many cases. If they have no prior history of bonding with your child, this process can be extremely challenging for some stepparents. Bonding with another person's children takes time. The children may not like their stepparents. The stepparent may not like the child.

A marital relationship can be challenging enough without children. Merging two families may be one of the most difficult things you will ever do. I only say this because I have seen so many examples where parents underestimated the time, commitment, and fortitude it would take to make this new blended family work. And if it does not work, your children's lives will be once again disrupted. You owe it to your children to take this process of dating and stepfamilies slowly.

Having a Child with Your New Partner

I have witnessed another concerning pattern in blended families. In some cases, once you have a child with your new partner, the first children you had from your previous relationship are seen as outsiders by your new partner. It can be especially hard for your new partner to bond with your children once they have their own child with you. Accepting your children from a previous relationship, once your new partner has a child with you, is a challenging situation for some stepparents. Your new partner may actually wish your kids did not exist. This is sad to me and so sad for your children from your previous relationship. Now, they have to live in a home where they feel unwelcome. These are some of the extreme cases I have seen. But, I want to make you fully aware of the reality and the potential consequences of dating and remarriage.

 ### Unhealthy Parent: Choosing a New Partner Who Is Not Healthy for You and/or Your Child

A mother called me saying her child was depressed and she believed it was due to her child's stepmother. I never believe one side of a story after this many years of working with parents. When I spoke with her teachers, they said Ava was a great kid, but had recently been acting very sad in school. Ava came into my office stating that her stepmom was mean and she did not feel her stepmom liked her. Ava told me she did not want to spend time at her dad's house because her stepmom was there. Ava said her stepmom always sided with her own daughter (from her previous marriage) and was always yelling at Ava. I had a session with Stepmom and Dad. Stepmom said, *"I just don't like her coming over to our house. I just don't like her."* No wonder this kid was depressed, she felt unwelcome in HER home. This stepmother had not welcomed this child into the home because of her own issues and now this child had to deal with the awful situation. We could assume her stepmom did not like Ava because she was from another mother she maybe did not like, or possibly they had to pay child support to Ava's mother, which was frustrating to her, but none of this was Ava's fault.

As I worked with Ava, I learned that she loved her dad so much and all she really wanted was to be able to spend time with him. Dad was stretched thin between his demanding new wife, two jobs, a new baby, and a new stepdaughter. This was not fair to his daughter.

Dad was confused because he and his new wife had a child together now. He was torn between staying with Stepmom (who was now the mother of his baby) and being a good dad to Ava. Ava was the one who lost out in this situation. The best I could do was recommend Dad see Ava without the stepmom around because it was clear his new wife was not going to change.

Shannon's Coaching: It is crucial to take new relationships slowly and ensure that your dating partners are good people. They must be able to accept one-hundred percent that you already have children. Time and time again, I see new stepparents not wanting to accept and embrace the FACT that you already had children before they entered the picture. Other people's children can be hard for a stepparent to fully accept.

Your child just wants time with you, their parent. You have to think about the children you already have when you are considering dating, stepfamilies, and having additional children. I ask you to make a choice right now to put your current children first as you re-enter the world of dating. They deserve this, period.

Ask Yourself: Should I really be dating right now? If I am dating, is this person able to one hundred percent (100%) accept the fact that a good portion of my time needs to be spent with my current child/children? Do they fully accept my current children and can I see a healthy relationship being built between this person and my children?

 ## Two Rules for Dating Prior to Introducing Your New Dating Partner to Your Child:

1. **It has been one year since you officially divorced or separated (separated means you have been living in different homes and your children know you are getting divorced).**

Why this is Important: Your children must go through the grief cycle before they are ready to meet anyone new in your life. The grief cycle is twelve to eighteen months. You also need time alone with your children to develop your relationship with them.

Child's Perspective: *"I feel like my dad is trying to replace my mom and I don't like that."* —Girl, age 8. Your kids have a mom and a dad; they don't need another new parent right now.

2. **You have dated your new dating partner for at least three months.**

Why this is Important: You must have time to assess this new partner before introducing them to your children. New dating partners can feel stressful to your child and you want to minimize the number of people you introduce to them. Children can get attached to new people and if the relationship then ends, they can feel another loss.

Child's Perspective: *"I did not have a mom in my life, so every time my dad brought someone home, I was sure she was going to be my new mommy, but usually after about three to six months she would leave and I would be heartbroken that my new mom left once again, this happened so many times in my life."* – Twenty-year-old female

Questions to Ask PRIOR to Introducing Your Children to Your Dating Partner

Complete the following exercise to help you assess possible red flags in a potential dating relationship. It will also assist you in assessing if you are ready to introduce your child to a new partner. These questions can be helpful if you are already dating and thinking about taking the next step.

Have I made it clear to my dating partner that my role as a parent is my first priority? Yes or No? If no, what do I need to do to be certain this is clearly understood?

_____

_____

_____

Does this person like children?

_____

_____

_____

Have I seen this person interacting positively with their own children (if they have them) and with other people's children?

_____

_____

_____

Why do I believe this person would be a positive role model for my child?

_____

_____

_____

Would I want this person to be a potential influence in my child's life?

_____

_____

_____

What do this person and I have in common and not have in common regarding our parenting views and parenting styles? Are they willing to take a parenting class with me so we can get on the same page?

_____

_____

_____

Have I dated this person for at least three to six months or feel fully committed to this person?

_____

_____

_____

Is this someone I could see myself committing to long-term? Why do I believe we would make a successful family unit?

_____

_____

_____

Have I had a discussion with this person about our possible future together?

_____

_____

_____

Do I know this person would agree to be a part of my family with my children?

_____

_____

_____

Does this dating partner approve of and understand my current relationship/situation with my child's other parent? Does my past relationship cause my new partner stress? If so, how might this impact our relationship and my children in the long-term?

_____

_____

_____

Will I still be able to fulfill my parenting time commitments if I date this person? If I live in the same area as my child's other parent, does the person I am dating want to stay in the same location (or within driving distance)? If they live somewhere else that would limit my time with my child if I moved there, are they willing to move to the general area where my children are until they are at least eighteen years of age?

_____

_____

_____

Have I been divorced, or in my child's mind, officially separated (the date your child knew their parents were no longer living together and you told them about the divorce) for at least a year?

_____

_____

_____

How does this relationship or person allow me to continue to put my child first?

_____

_____

_____

Do I believe in my heart that my child/children are emotionally ready to be introduced to someone else? Why or why not?

_____

_____

_____

Your answers to these important questions will help you to determine if you are ready to introduce your child to the person you are dating. If you don't feel ready to discuss these questions with your dating partner, you are definitely not ready to introduce your children to them. You are also not ready for the next step in the relationship. Take your time; it is important to proceed with confidence in your choices. Always remember you are a parent first.

 ## What Would You Do?

You have met someone wonderful and you tell them you have your child fifty percent (50%) of the time. You tell your new dating partner that you can only see them every other week for the first three months (you have your child every other week). You tell them you can talk to them at night and if something important is happening during the week, you have your children you can possibly get a babysitter. This new person looks at you and says, "I am not sure I can handle that. I would miss you and I need to see you more than that."

ANSWER:

Set a boundary and say, "no." This will clearly demonstrate to your new potential partner that you are a parent first. See if they positively respond. If not, RUN (big red flag: they cannot be alone, they may be codependent, they could be jealous of your child in the long-term, or they will not understand you are a parent first). Be grateful you saw this early.

 ## Healthy Parent: Building a Healthy Bond with Your Children and Dating Responsibly

Jessie's dad took dating slowly. He knew his kids came first and he even told them that. He knew it was his job as a father to protect his growing children from anyone who may not be a good role model for them in their life. He took a full year to FIRST build his relationship with his children after the divorce. They became a close family. After this bonding period with his children, he started to take some time when he did not have the kids to date. Once he had dated the same woman for six months, he felt ready to introduce her to his kids. He introduced her slowly and still made sure to spend at least fifty percent (50%) of his time alone with his children without his new partner present. He once again told his kids they were number one and made that very clear to his new partner. She was fine with it because she had her own friends and life. She thought he was a great dad because of it and loved him more for it. He also warned her that his kids may frustrate her and they would have to deal with that as a family at times. He made sure she was positive with his children and his children easily adjusted to the new situation with no issues. His children thanked him later in life for putting them first.

Ask Yourself: What is my plan for dating and how will I be sure to put my kids first?

✚ Emergency Parenting Tip: Dating

If you are currently in a new relationship, take a moment and assess how much time you spend with your child versus your dating partner when you have your parenting time with your children. Increase your time alone (without your new partner) with your children. To your child, this time with you is GOLD.

STEP #7
TAKE CARE OF YOU AND LOVE YOURSELF— IT TAKES A HEALTHY PARENT TO RAISE HEALTHY CHILDREN

 Ensuring that you are as healthy as possible is the foundational piece to being a great parent after divorce for your child.

Research shows that if one parent is a solid, healthy parent, it minimizes the overall risk for kids.

This fact, in my opinion, is the biggest reason of all for you to get healthy in your life. If you can't get healthy for you, choose to get healthy for your child. When you are on an airplane, they say in the safety warning, in case of a loss of cabin pressure "secure your own oxygen mask first." Once you take care of yourself, you will then be able to better care for your child. You are your children's mirror. They will be as healthy as you are.

 Unhealthy Parenting: Serial Dating Without Self-Love

Sue's mom was a true single parent. Her dad had never been in her life for physical or financial support. Sue's mom had a need to be with someone all the time. She was very codependent and looked to men to make her feel happy (which will never work). Sue reported to me that every six months, her mom would start a new relationship. She would introduce the man to Sue immediately. Since Sue had no father figure in her life, she looked at every one of these men as her new daddy. However, once her mom realized this guy also was not going to make her happy, he was always gone within six months. This was so confusing for Sue and every time she was sure she did something wrong. The only thing she knew was that none of her daddy's loved her. This provided Sue with a very low level of confidence. She married young and was divorced in a couple of years.

Shannon's Coaching: It is imperative to provide stability for your children. Bringing in someone new every six months is detrimental to your children. This mother needs to take time to find out more about loving herself. Spending quality time with herself and her daughter is much more important than desperately trying to find a new partner at any cost. If Mom takes time to become healthier, she will attract a healthier partner who may end up staying with her and her daughter.

Ask Yourself: Do you need to take some time to focus on self-love right now and become healthier so you can attract a healthier partner?

Health is comprised of many factors. Take a moment now and assess your current health status and commit to what you can do to increase your overall health for yourself and your child.

 ## Assess Your Level of Self-Care

Review the chart below. Select the number that best reflects your behavior and agreement with the statements below.

(1=Low/Never   5=Moderate/Sometimes   10=Yes/High)

FOOD: The food I eat is healthy for me (fruits, vegetables, proteins, healthy fats, low sugar). 1	2	3	4	5	6	7	8	9	10
DRINK: The drink I consume is healthy for me (low, no sugar). 1	2	3	4	5	6	7	8	9	10
STRESS: I have healthy ways to release and cope with stress. 1	2	3	4	5	6	7	8	9	10
EXERCISE: I have a healthy exercise plan of 3-5 times per week. 1	2	3	4	5	6	7	8	9	10

RELATIONSHIPS: I have kind, healthy, and supportive people in my life.	1	2	3	4	5	6	7	8	9	10
SUPPORT: I have good networks of friends, family, and other support groups.	1	2	3	4	5	6	7	8	9	10
EMOTIONAL: I feel stable enough to effectively parent my child.	1	2	3	4	5	6	7	8	9	10

Action:

For any categories (in the previous section) where you rated yourself lower than a five, make a commitment now to improve those areas. Write in the space below (in the table) what you need to do to improve these areas.

FOOD: The food I eat is healthy for me (fruits, vegetables, proteins, healthy fats).	
DRINK: The drink I consume is healthy for me.	
STRESS: I have healthy ways to release stress.	
EXERCISE: I have a healthy exercise plan of 3-5 times per week.	
RELATIONSHIPS: I have kind and healthy people in my life.	
SUPPORT: I have good networks of friends, family, and other support groups.	

EMOTIONAL:	
I feel stable enough to effectively parent my child.	

Now, assess everything you wrote above. Write down one to two goals you know you want to focus on in the next week.

_____

_____

_____

 ## Never Underestimate the Power of Loving Yourself

Growing up in a family with constant anger and fighting, I had no idea how to love myself. In my relationships, I recreated what I had experienced in my family (fighting, anger, disconnection). Though I desperately wanted a happy, loving, and peaceful family, I had absolutely no idea how to create one . After many failures, I set out to find out how I could be a healthy partner and parent. What I discovered was the key to healthy relationships was to love myself first.

If you don't love yourself, it can be very challenging to love your child or partner in a healthy way. Give your child this gift and increase your level of self-love. In my book: *In Love with Me: Ten Steps to Self-Love and Successful Relationships*, http://bit.ly/2017ilwm-book you can learn about many ways to do this. I have also created best-selling, guided meditation CDs that assisted me and have helped many others in building their self-love through loving, guided visualizations: *The Healing Journey Within: Meditations for Abundance and Love Volume I: Deserving* and *Volume II: Worthiness. http://inlovewithme.com/meditations*. These meditations focus on developing that deep foundational love we all need to create peace in our lives and in our families.

To assist you in beginning this journey of self-love, the first step you can take is to receive my gift to you, my Heart-Opening Guided Meditation (from Volume I of my CDs). You can access it via this link: http://bit.ly/heartopen

📖 Cultivate Self Love

1. Do I realize I am the only person who can truly make me happy? No one else actually *makes* us unhappy. It is a choice.

_____

_____

_____

2. What kind of life and love do I deserve?

_____

_____

_____

3. What step can I take to move forward to create my new life of love?

_____

_____

_____

📖 Connect to Yourself with Simple Meditation

This simple meditation allows you to be more present and calm. Try it now.

1. Close your eyes.
2. Take three deep breaths, in through your nose, out through your mouth.
3. Let your body relax.
4. Move your body to release tension.
5. Sit for three more breaths or however long you would like.
6. Say to yourself, "I let go of anything I don't need right now."
7. Take one more deep breath and as you let it out, let go.
8. Say to yourself, "I receive in everything I need at this moment." Breathe, envision your heart opening, and receive all that you need with each breath.
9. Take two more deep breaths.

Now, say these words aloud to yourself:

I love myself because I deserve it. No matter what has happened in my past, I have done my best. I choose to be patient and kind with myself. I acknowledge all I have been through in this life. I also acknowledge myself for all I have accomplished. I am a beautiful person. I deserve the best life possible and so do my amazing children. I am so grateful I have this gift of my child(ren) in my life. I am going to take the important steps each day to put myself first and be healthy for my kids and me. As I love myself, I will be able to love my children in a healthy way.

STEP #8
TELLING CHILDREN YOU ARE DIVORCING AND NAVIGATING PARENTING TIME SCHEDULES

The best route to take in telling your children you and your spouse are divorcing/ separating is to be honest with them without sharing intimate details and/or subjective emotional opinions about what happened. Telling children can be one of the most difficult conversations you will have with them.

Consider These Items before Telling Your Child You Are Divorcing

1. **Make Sure This Decision is Final.** Ensure that this is a final decision, you have done all you are going to do to make your marriage work, and you now know the only alternative is divorce. This does not always mean both parents want the divorce, but it means you are sure there are no other options for your family right now. It is hard for children when parents go back and forth, so be sure about your decision before you tell the children.

   Ask Yourself: Do I believe in my heart this is a final decision (or do I know my co-parent knows this is a final decision)?

2. **Am I Stable Enough to Have This Conversation?** Ask yourself if you are emotionally stable enough to be there for your child in this meeting. This meeting can set the stage for the rest of this divorce process. Your child needs you right now. Your job in this conversation is to focus on the needs of your child and be available for their concerns, questions, and emotions.

   Ask Yourself: Have I processed my own emotions enough so I can be emotionally stable in this meeting with my children?

3. **Don't Make Promises You Can't Keep.** It is important in this conversation to not make promises that you cannot keep. This can be a challenge because things change. Be realistic with your words and promises. Children remember promises and this can undermine trust later. If you don't know something, be honest with your child.

Ask Yourself: What might my kids ask about (school, home, dog, time with each parent) and am I certain I won't make any promises I can't keep?

4. **Reasons for the Divorce.** It can be difficult to explain to your children the reason for your separation or divorce. Parents always want to know what is best to tell their children. Some things may be too much for them to hear at this time and would be better addressed in the future. This is true in cases of infidelity, drug/alcohol usage, etc. Never in this meeting should one person be blamed. This will not be helpful to your child during this difficult conversation. The simple way to say it is, "We no longer make each other happy and we can't meet each other's needs." In most cases, I also believe it is best that both parties take responsibility for the marriage ending. Most therapists agree that both spouses have contributed to the marital break-up. I would suggest looking at your part in the relationship ending and see if it seems right to share this with your children—again, without sharing intimate details. If you both agree this has been one parent's choice, more than the other parent's, then you can tell this to the child. You still want to be careful to not blame that person, but if they want to accept responsibility for the choice that is fine. I do believe in being honest (to a point) with your child because not being honest can undermine their trust later. However, again, there should be no intimate details shared.

Ask Yourself: Am I prepared to answer the question "why?" and be responsible for my part in what happened without sharing intimate details or blaming?

5. **Where to Tell Them.** Next, decide where and when you will tell your children. In the home is usually best and it should certainly not be in a public place. You want them to be able to go to their room to comfort themselves. If at all possible, don't tell them right near bedtime. Also, don't tell them if one parent is planning on going out of town the next day. Be available for your child for at least a week after the initial conversation.

Ask Yourself: Have we decided where we will tell the kids? Is this a safe place for them to experience their emotions?

6. **Tell Them Together.** If possible, tell your children together. Both parents should be there and all of your children should be present. This is best because both parents are there to respond to your children's questions. It also reassures your children that this is a decision both of you have been involved in. You may have to make some age-appropriate choices in the words you use, but if the kids are all together, they will all hear the same message, which is important. You can talk with them individually after the conversation if they have further questions.

Ask Yourself: Are we able to take the high road and do this together for the good of our children? If we have already told them separately, can we have another discussion with the kids where both parents are present?

7. **Showing Emotion.** It is okay to cry. Parents think they have to be strong, but this belief is not necessarily true. If you cry, your child feels it is okay for them to cry, too. I do not recommend crying the entire time or crying so much that you can't talk. Some emotion is good, excessive emotion is not during this conversation. If you find yourself in the place of not being able to stop crying when you tell your children, excuse yourself for a few minutes, go to the bathroom, take some deep breaths, tell yourself you can do this, and return to your children. They need your strength right now. If you know this will be difficult for you, I encourage you to take time and cry prior to the meeting on your own. This will assist you in processing so that you can be calmer in front of your children. Remember, your children rely on you for safety and security. If they sense you feel unsafe, this will create additional stress for your child. If the discussion gets angry or someone is very upset, take a time out and say you will get back together in a few minutes. If the other parent happens to blame you, work to remain calm and let your children know that divorce can make people upset.

Ask Yourself: Do I know it is okay to have tears and show emotion, but not react in a way that will make my children worry about me or feel unsafe?

8. **Who Will Begin?** Decide who will start out the conversation with your children. You should take turns if possible. Only say what is honest for you.

Ask Yourself: Have we agreed who will begin the conversation?

9. **What Do You Know for Certain?** Decide what you know for certain and will tell the children. Know this before you go into the meeting with your children (e.g., mom/dad will live in an apartment; the kids will live at (location) and go to the same school for the rest of this year). Make sure you write these out and agree on these before the meeting with the children.

Ask Yourself: What are the facts we know for certain about logistics?

10. **Positive Attitude.** Attitude is everything. If you think that you can do this in a healthy way, you will do this in a healthy way. Create your intention for this meeting. This intention could be: calm, clear communication with love.

Ask Yourself: What is my positive intention for this meeting with my kids?

Parenting Time Schedules

This is a very emotional issue for both parents. Remember it is best for your children to have a relationship with both parents, if possible. The thoughts I have on parenting time schedules include the following:

- There is no perfect parenting plan. The perfect plan is the one that works the best for your family. Hundreds of examples online can possibly fit your situation. Come up with a few ideas and discuss them with your co-parent and your children (if they are old enough).

- Children NEVER get to make any final decision on parenting time. They can give their thoughts and then parents or judges make the final decision. You never want them to have guilt over any decision they feel they made, ever.

- Consistency is the key. Make a plan and stay with it the best you can. Inform your children as far ahead of time as you can about any changes.

- You and your co-parent are in charge of your plan. Once you decide on your plan, you can decide to be flexible; the courts don't have to sign off. Of course, this is only if the two of you have a decent relationship. It still would be good to get changes detailed in an email or document. You decide if you need to change the documents and file again with the courts.

- Do not punish your children for your decision to divorce. Punishing them regarding the plan looks like this, "You cannot go to your best friend's birthday party this weekend because it is my weekend and I won't drive forty-five minutes to bring you there." Your child should still be able to do most of the things they would have been able to do if you lived under the same roof with your co-parent.

- If you have teenagers, yes it can be nice to give them some more control to decide where they want to be on a certain night. However, there should still be a structured schedule that is followed eighty percent (80%) of the time so they have the opportunity to build a relationship with both of you.

- Be as flexible as you can with your co-parent. If they are finally deciding to step up and be the parent you always wished they would be, be grateful that you chose someone who wants to be a parent to your children. It is very important your children have both of you in their lives if possible.

- Do not over promise and under deliver. You need to be realistic about the time you can spend with your children. If you agree to see them every weekend and you are working out of town and only end up getting back every other weekend, you need to revise your plan. You let your kids down if they are expecting time with you that does not happen. This is not fair to your children.

- Some parents become very frustrated if feel they do not receive enough time with their children. Always remember it is the quality of time you spend with your children vs the quantity of time.
- If you had the opportunity to stay home with your children (a decision you both made together) do not use this as a reason to now punish your co-parent by demanding that you continue to have significantly more time with your children. If your co-parent now wants fifty percent (50%) of the time, consider that it is important for your children to have a solid relationship with both of you. I will never forget one parent who this happened to, her co-parent took her to court and won more time with the children because he had been the parent the family had decided would stay home and he had built a stronger relationship with the children. She wanted this opportunity to spend more time with her girls to build her relationship with them. She said to me, "His girlfriend now sees my girls more than I do." Allow your co-parent to be a parent if they want to.
- The plan may need to change as your child grows, be flexible.

 ## Unhealthy Parenting: No Consistency with Parenting Plan

Phillip's mom and dad wanted to be flexible with their plan. Phillip's dad had moved about three hours away and they agreed he could see Phillip on the weekends when he wanted, which was averaging about a weekend every couple of months. They had no set weekends. When Phillip came to see me he was feeling a lot of anxiety because he did not know when he would see his dad next and he was worried about not seeing his dad ever again. This was causing Phillip to act out and he actually had begun sipping some of his mom's alcohol to "hopefully relax and feel better." Phillip was twelve years old.

Shannon's Coaching: Kids need consistency in their parenting time schedule with both parents. It is very important to make sure your children know when they will be having parenting time with each of you. Making a calendar that they can visually see can be very helpful and having one of these at each home is important.

Ask Yourself: Do we need more consistency for our children in our parenting time schedule?

Shared parenting can seem challenging for everyone involved. However, I have some good news. Recent studies have shown that kids report that shared parenting was fine because it allowed them to build a relationship with both of their parents. This is good news for everyone.

STEP #9
SET HEALTHY BOUNDARIES—WITH YOUR CHILD AND CO-PARENT

When we set healthy boundaries or limits, we feel safe and secure, and healthy relationships are the result. You may not consciously realize when your boundaries are being crossed in an unhealthy way or even when you are crossing others' boundaries in an unhealthy way. This type of behavior may be all you have ever experienced. You may have grown up in an environment with unhealthy boundaries where you did not feel fully safe. You may have been in a situation where your boundaries were continuously violated, often without you even realizing it. Even if your parents did everything for you and/or allowed you to do whatever you wanted, they also modeled unhealthy boundaries to you.

At this point, it is very important to focus on setting healthy boundaries with your co-parent and your child. Families that cannot set healthy boundaries usually have some form of co-dependency occurring within the family. They enable each other to continue unhealthy behaviors versus supporting each other to become stronger through healthy boundaries, structures, and rules.

Healthy Boundaries with Your Co-Parent

This can be tricky because you may not have had good boundaries with your co-parent before the divorce. If you did not have children together, you would never have to see this other person again. If your child was not present, you could simply go your own way and heal on your own. Your child now holds the two of you together in some way. Your child is the lynchpin that holds you together and (hopefully) the catalyst for positive change. You have to continue to see each other and communicate with each other, which can be a challenge for some couples. It is challenging because possibly the sound of your voice or seeing you brings up all your co-parent's old insecurities and makes them angry and/or sad. Time apart begins the healing so you both can move on, but when you see each other again, the old wounds can be reopened. It is important to give yourselves some time and space to heal. The best way to give yourselves time to heal is to set good boundaries. The following strategies are for co-parents who are having a hard time communicating respectfully and/or setting healthy boundaries.

Boundary Strategies for Your Co-Parent

1. **One parent drops the kids off somewhere (school, Grandma's) and then the other picks them up.** This is a very healthy option if seeing your co-parent is conflict-provoking or stressful initially. All police stations will provide this service for free if you need that.

2. **Minimize your phone conversations.** Do more texting and emailing for now. Less contact speeds up the healing process so you can both move forward.

3. **You never have to listen to anyone yell at you on the phone or in person.** You can either hang up or excuse yourself. Do not get into the negative energy with your co-parent. Take care of yourself. Most likely, the kids are with one of you and no one should be exposed to this kind of negative communication.

4. **Decide on the protocol for drop-offs.** If your child is old enough, let them walk into the other parent's home without you. If the two of you are in any kind of conflict during the exchange of your children, it is stressful for your child.

5. **Do not let rude emails entice you.** If your co-parent is sending mean, angry emails, it means they are feeling terrible inside. Misery loves company. Humans only say mean things when we feel really upset and awful toward ourselves. If you respond, you give them what they want—this negative connection with you. Remember, they win this game if you respond to them. Over time, if you truly ignore them, and they are not reinforced for this bad behavior, it will stop. This may take a while, but it is the law of human behavior. They will get bored if they do not get their "fix" of hearing from you.

 ## Assess Your Boundaries with Your Co-Parent

Did I experience unhealthy boundaries as a child? Do I see any of this re-created with my co-parent?

_____

_____

_____

What do I need to do to set better boundaries with my co-parent?

_____

_____

_____

 # Healthy Boundaries, Structures, and Rules with Your Children

Working with children early in my career, I recognized right away that boundaries, structures, and rules made them feel safe and secure.

The truth is that your child's life can be at stake if you do not choose to set healthy and safe boundaries for them. I have seen kids end up in harm's way due to their parents' lack of boundaries with them, especially during the teenage years. Sometimes children of divorce get to do many more things than they would have if their parents lived together. Some parents let kids do what they want to try to win them over or out of their own guilt. These are not healthy reasons to allow your children the ability to take early risks. If you do not set healthy boundaries for your children, you are putting them at risk for:

- underage drinking
- driving while under the influence
- doing drugs
- being a teen parent
- unsafe behaviors (cutting, hurting themselves, internet addictions)
- poor school performance

Important: *The above are all risks for your children if you don't set boundaries when they are with you and agree with your co-parent on curfews and rules for your children.*

The bottom line: *Rules and boundaries help your children feel cared about. They make your child feel safe and secure. They help your child make healthier choices. They may resist them, but know deep down they know this is in their best interest.*

As a parent coach, I have seen many parents struggle in this area. Usually, one parent is lenient. From my perspective, that parent is usually co-dependent with their kids and treating them more like their friend. This truly leads to an unfortunate situation for all. Children don't learn to be responsible adults in this type of environment.

The lenient parent can also undermine the other parent's relationship with the kids. This happens because the parent who sets rules and boundaries is not the parent teenagers usually like, especially if they have a lenient "friend" parent. They think the parent that has structure is mean; thus, it undermines the relationship with this parent. The truth is kids thrive on rules and boundaries. They also thrive when the two of you communicate about them.

Your Personal Boundaries with Your Child: Is Your Child Taking Care of You?

Ask yourself the following questions (check yes or no):

	Yes	No
Is my child reassuring me that things will be okay?	☐	☐
Does my child sacrifice their own fun to stay by my side?	☐	☐
Do I ask my child for advice?	☐	☐
Is my child doing chores and things they did not do prior to the divorce, which may not be appropriate for their age?	☐	☐
Does my child spend time caretaking me and making me feel better on a regular or even semi-regular basis?	☐	☐
I do **not** have at least one or two friends whom I regularly spend time with.	☐	☐
Have I told my child information about their other parent they do not need to hear?	☐	☐
Have I seen a look of worry on my child's face when I have told them something?	☐	☐
Do I tell my child details about my dating/love life that I would normally share with a friend?	☐	☐
Do I treat my child more as a friend than as a child who should not hear intimate details about their parent's life?	☐	☐
Do I regularly tell my child my problems, worries or fears?	☐	☐
Do I expect my child to do things with me that I really should be doing with friends?	☐	☐

If you answered "*Yes*" to any of the questions above, you do NOT have healthy boundaries with your children.

It is crucial to stop using your child for these purposes and obtain support from others. When you do not set healthy boundaries with your children you rob them of their childhood because they don't get to be kids. Instead, they worry about you and take care of you, which is not fair to them.

If you checked any of the boxes above, take a few minutes now to write down what you will do to set better boundaries with your children.

_____

_____

_____

What one action can you take to bring other methods of support (other than your children) into your life (groups, friends, church, family)?

_____

_____

_____

Please read the following statement out loud to yourself:

Using my child to support me during this time is not fair to them. I am standing in the way of my child's healthy growth and development. I will find my own resources to support me through this process.

 ## Your Child as Your Best Friend

Do you ever say your child is your best friend? Is it okay to say this? My perspective is it is too big of a responsibility for your child to be your best friend. It is as paramount for your children to have their own friends as it is for you to have your own friends. One dad I worked with said his father was his friend as a kid and he felt he missed out on having a "father" telling him what he was doing was right. He really missed having a father figure as a kid. Kids also may not respect you if they see you as their friend. Setting and enforcing rules and boundaries will most likely be challenging. Not having boundaries can lead to your children engaging in at-risk behaviors.

Unhealthy Parents: No Communication Regarding Healthy Boundaries for Kids

Haley and Jenna were 14 and 17 when their parents separated. Mom and Dad were not communicating well after the divorce. Mom was very lenient with the girls now that she was out on her own and separated from Dad. Dad had reasonable rules in his home for curfews and overnights with friends/boyfriends. Mom and Dad could not agree on curfews and overnights. Mom thought the girls should be able to do what they wanted and she was friends with them for the most part. The girls began to stay at Mom's house more frequently. They liked their freedom; they were teenagers! Dad became frustrated that his daughters would not uphold his rules even if they were with Mom. He stopped communicating with his oldest daughter. At this point, the oldest daughter, who was a star basketball player, showed up at a school football game drunk. These girls were not headed on a good path, all due to their parents' inability to communicate and set healthy boundaries together for their children.

Shannon's Coaching: Kids need boundaries and rules. When two parents don't communicate and agree on rules for their children, kids have full control. This can put your children at a high threat for at-risk behaviors (drugs, alcohol, teen pregnancies, gangs, etc.). Being friends with your children and being too lenient in the hopes your children will like you more is not healthy parenting. Mom should look into codependency and seek out her own counseling. The parents should work with a professional or another successful family to see what rules they had for their children and agree to implement those rules.

Ask Yourself: Can my co-parent and I agree on healthy rules and boundaries for our children? If we can't, is it important to seek support to ensure we do communicate about and agree on these very important issues for the health of our children?

 ## Setting Boundaries for Your Children

1. Are you being too lenient and acting more like a friend to your children?

_____

_____

_____

2. What structure do you know you need to provide for your child to ensure their safety and security?

_____

_____

_____

3. What do you and your co-parent need to do to get on the same page about rules and boundaries for your kids?

_____

_____

_____

4. What could happen your kids if you don't work together to set healthy boundaries for your children?

_____

_____

_____

Strategies for Setting Boundaries and Rules (for Your Children) with Your Co-Parent

1. Find someone you both trust who has raised healthy children. Ask what their rules were and adopt some of those rules for your kids.

2. Agree to follow the recommendations of a family therapist.

3. Agree to mediate if you just can't reach an agreement yourselves.

As you can see, boundaries play a crucial part in your success as a co-parent and a parent. If you believe you and your co-parent do not have healthy boundaries I strongly recommend reading further on co-dependency. Boundaries help us create healthy relationships, which will benefit you and your children for the rest of your lives.

STEP #10
CONNECTION WITH YOUR CHILD

 Ask any child. All they want is focused, loving, quality time with you. They want your love and attention more than anything else. They want you to connect with them in a healthy way.

 Unhealthy Parent: Allowing Your Anger Regarding Your Amount of Parenting Time to Impact Your Relationship with Your Children

Jillian's dad, Joe did not receive the amount of parenting time he wanted with his children. He received only three days every other weekend. He was upset at the judge and at his co-parent. Unfortunately for his children, Joe took this anger out on his kids. He would cancel his parenting time with his children to attend events with his girlfriend. He would call his co-parent at the last minute and have her tell the children he would not be coming to their parenting time. His daughter, Jillian, came into see me because she was sad and cutting herself. Her father had been canceling his parenting time and she was extremely sad. She told me that since the divorce she did not have a good relationship with her father. She also told me, "I want him to tell me if he is not going to be at my parenting time, I don't want him to tell my mom." This little girl was so sad that her dad was abandoning her due to his anger at a decision she had nothing to do with. She loved him very much and felt a huge loss due to his behavior.

Shannon's Coaching: Remember it is the quality versus quantity of time you spend with your children. One parent may be awarded more time, but they may be on their phone the entire time or focusing on their new partner. Take the time you receive and make the choice to spend healthy and loving quality time building strong relationships with your children. Be grateful for the time you do have with your children.

Ask Yourself: Do I have any anger about the amount of time I have with my children? Can I choose to let my anger go and instead enjoy and be grateful for the time I do have with my precious children?

Suggestions for Listening to and Connecting with Your Child

- During a percentage of your parenting time, put away any distractions so you can completely focus on your child. Shut off your cell phone, move away from the computer, and do whatever is necessary to remove any distractions. Have your child do the same.
- Take a deep breath so you can be present with your child; clear your mind of other thoughts. Have an open heart and mind. Say to yourself, "I am here for my child."
- Face your child squarely and be at their level. Sit on the floor with them if that is where they are.
- Look into your child's eyes with pure love.
- If they are going through something, ask your child questions, for example, "How does that make you feel? How are you doing today?"
- Empathize with your child. "Seems like you are feeling..." e.g., sad, angry, or frustrated. Or simply, "How are you feeling?" Don't put your opinions on them or assume they are feeling a certain way. Don't offer solutions unless they ask for them.
- Physically connect with your child to show them you love them. Give your child a hug or a pat on the back. You can also tell them verbally how much you love them. If appropriate, you can say how proud you are of them or how much confidence you have in them that they can make good choices.
- Give your child a compliment about something they have recently done well.

 ## Connect with Your Children

When you are with your child how much time do you spend time focused just on them, and how much time do you spend focusing on many other things at the same time (or maybe just your phone)?

How much of your parenting time do you focus only on your child? Circle the percentage below.

10% 20% 30% 40% 50% 60% 70% 80% 90% 100%

1. What one thing can you commit to so you can increase this percentage by ten percent (10%)?

   _____

   _____

   _____

2. How much time do you spend asking your children questions, playing games, going on walks, doing things just with your family, singing together in the car, giving them hugs, telling them how awesome they are, and holding your kids (depending on age)?

   _____

   _____

   _____

3. What can you commit to the next time you are with your child to connect with, listen to and show them that you love them? What will you do differently?

   _____

   _____

   _____

Remember, your child will grow up and you will not have the opportunity to replace the days, weeks, and years. I ask you now to make a choice to be fully present with yourself and your child. Give them this gift of your loving presence. It is a key factor to children's health.

 ## Connect at Bedtime

Before bedtime, spend five to ten minutes with each child going over their day and celebrating their successes, or "prouds" as one young boy called it. Take this time with your child each day, it means so much to them. You can do this with children of all ages. I have done it with my daughter since she was two months old.

Stay Connected: Parenting Time

Do not let the fact that you did not get the amount of time with your children you wanted affect your attitude and parenting time with your children. Use what time you have to be the best parent possible for your kids. One parent may have the kids for seventy percent (70%), but if they are not present with the kids and always doing other things, this is not quality time. If you have thirty percent (30%) and **you are present and doing quality activities with your children, this time could actually be more valuable to your kids than the time with your co-parent who has 70% (if they are not present to your children).**

You can choose to spend additional time with your children at other events and occasions. Below are some ideas you can implement to have more time with your children:

- Coach their sports teams
- Volunteer with their school's PTA
- Volunteer in their classroom
- Volunteer to chaperone school events
- Lead any activity they are part of (i.e. Girl Scouts or Boy Scouts leader)
- If your co-parent needs a babysitter after school, see if you can work out your schedule to take care of your child after school during your co-parent's parenting time (they must agree to this).
- Create special one-on-one time with you and each of your children.

 Healthy Parent: Finding Creative Ways to Spend Quality Time with Your Children

Sharon did not receive the amount of parenting time she wanted with her girls. She received three days every other week. She was very sad about that. She finally realized that the only thing she could do was be the best parent possible to her children when she was with them. She also took the time away from her children to get healthy herself. She attended parenting classes and took some classes to help further her career. She talked to her kids' teachers at the beginning of the year and volunteered in each child's classroom each week. She volunteered for every field trip she could. She also became the troop leader of her daughters' Girl Scouts group so she saw her daughters each week. Her daughters saw her as a strong, confident, and happy mother.

Shannon's Coaching: This situation was not the life Sharon had imagined, but she made a choice to make the best of it. She took every step possible to ensure she was a positive part of her daughters' lives. Her daughters grew up knowing their mom loved them very much which was the best gift she could give them.

Ask Yourself: What can I do to be move involved in my child's life outside of my parenting time?

You must practice connecting with your child. *Connection is the most priceless gift you will EVER give your child.*

EMBRACING THE FUTURE:
YOU CAN DO THIS!

In this final section, I want to provide you with the "Parent's Promise," a document created by children of divorce for children of divorce. If you keep these promises, you are sure to raise happy and healthy children of divorce.

 Commit to the Parent's Promise

Written by Children of Divorce for Parents of Divorce

For the greatest good of my child, I hereby agree that:

1.) I will not speak negatively about my child's other parent to my child.
2.) I will not say to my child, "That (*insert negative behavior or characteristic*) is just like your father/mother."
3.) I agree not to put my child in the middle of issues I have with the other parent (especially child support).
4.) I agree not to use my child as a pawn to get back at their other parent.
5.) I agree that if my child's other parent has a new relationship; I will not speak negatively of this other person to my child.
6.) I will not expect my child to take care of me when I am upset.
7.) I will periodically ask my child how he or she is doing.
8.) I will do my best to support my child fully during this process.
9.) I will allow my child to be a child during this time.
10.) I will seek outside professional counseling if I need to speak with someone about this situation or if I am having difficulty maintaining this agreement.
11.) I agree that if I do not uphold the above promises that I personally am not acting in the best interest of my child's physical and emotional health.

> BY AGREEING TO THE PARENT'S PROMISE, I AM ACCEPTING RESPONSI-
> BILITY AS A PARENT TO PROVIDE THE BEST ENVIRONMENT POSSIBLE
> DURING THIS TRANSITION FOR MY CHILD.
>
> IN UPHOLDING THIS PROMISE, I ALSO ACKNOWLEDGETO MY CHILD
> THAT THEY HAVE NO FAULT IN THE DECISION MADE BY THEIR PARENTS.
> I AM FULLY COMMITTED TO THE BEST INTEREST OF MY CHILD'S EMO-
> TIONAL AND PHYSICAL HEALTH DURING THIS TIME AND TO THEIR FU-
> TURE GROWTH AND DEVELOPMENT.
>
> Honestly and with much love, I commit to this for my child's sake.
>
> Signature: _____

Envision Your Child's Wedding (or Other Important Life Event)

See yourself in the future at your child's wedding. It's a beautiful day, the ceremony was wonderful, and your child is so happy. Feel the love you have for your child that they have chosen this wonderful partner and are content. You are seated at the family table at the wedding reception with your co-parent. You are being respectful and sharing in the joy of raising this beautiful child. Feel this feeling of gratitude toward your co-parent for allowing you to bring this child into the world. Thank your co-parent for the way the two of you successfully worked together for the best interest of your child.

This future vision is your goal.

Focus on Your Children's Future

Take two deep breaths. Feel all the love you have inside your heart for your children, when you hug them or when you feel so proud of them. Take a deep breath and get really connected to that love. Close your eyes if you'd like.

Now, envision them ten (if older kids) or twenty years (if younger kids) into the future. They are grown up. They are happy and healthy. They are peaceful with their families and friends. Feel the joy inside of you that they are doing so well. Feel how proud you are of their success. Take a deep breath as you take this in; you were successful as a parent.

Now, see them walking up to you. What do they say to you? What do they thank you for as a parent and co-parent that made their life easy and peace-filled? What actions did you take that made this journey easier for them?

Know you can do these things for your children. Write the things your children would tell you here:

_____

_____

_____

 ## The Future of Our Children, the Future of Our World

In closing, I want to leave you with this poem……

> *Let all of us, in our own unique way, recommit ourselves to the search for the pebbles of change that can be cast into the social pond. Let us create a divorce process that recycles divorce pain into new patterns of personal and familial growth which, in turn, will also strengthen our entire society. Let us protect our children from the unnecessary hazards of the divorce experience so that they, like their parents, can be strengthened by divorce rather than defeated by it. And, let us never forget that if the lights go out in our children's eyes, be they children of divorce or any other children, we will all live in darkness.*
>
> —Meyer Elkin, Editor AFCC

****

I wish you and your children all the very best. I know you can do this and one day your children will thank you for taking this path that is sometimes less traveled. They will thank you either personally or by the healthy and happy lives and relationships they create.

With Love and Peace,
Shannon R Rios Paulsen, MS LMFT
www.healthychildrenofdivorce.com
www.inlovewithme.com
www.manifestingbaby.com
www.rioscoaching.com

Continuing Your Learning: Take Action for Your Children

You must take the next step to ensure your learning is carried out in your life. As adults, if we don't use it, we lose it. I recommend taking time now to decide what you will do to put structure into your life to commit to the crucial actions you identified in this book. You may want to put the Parent's Promise up on your refrigerator or door. You may want to post a sticky note with a reminder somewhere. You may want to read a book on any of the topics I covered that you know you need further understanding of. Whatever it is, take that action. Seeking support and guidance is strength, not weakness.

If you believe you would benefit from continuing to work with me in some way to ensure your success in this journey, I have created the following opportunities for you at a discounted rate (only available to those that purchased this book):

Self-Love Resources

FREE — Heart-Opening Guided Meditation:
Shannon lovingly guides you to listen to messages of your heart.
http://inlovewithme.com/heart-opening-meditation-free-gift

FREE — Receiving Questionnaire:
Download the Receiving questionnaire to assess how well you receive and learn to receive more in your life.
http://inlovewithme.com

Life Coaching Sessions:
Take your life to the next level! Working one-on-one with Shannon is a priceless gift to yourself. Use coupon code **lifedeal** to receive a 25% discount on life coaching sessions.
http://inlovewithme.com/life-coaching

Guided Meditations:
The Healing Journey Within: Meditations for Abundance and Love: Volume I (Deserving) & Volume II (Manifesting) by Shannon Rios MS LMFT
Give yourself this gift of deepening your self-love.
2 for 1: Download one and get the other free.
http://inlovewithme.com/two-for-one
OR
Amazon (hard copy or download):
Volume I: http://bit.ly/selflovemedvol1
Volume II: http://bit.ly/selflovemedvol2

Self-Love Book:
In Love With Me: Ten Steps to Self-Love and Successful Relationships by Shannon R Rios Paulsen, MS, LMFT.
Download is 50% off the cover price.
http://bit.ly/loveme7
OR
Amazon (hard copy or download): http://bit.ly/10stepsselflovebook

Motherhood & Fertility Coaching/Book:
Shannon coaches women whose dream is to become mothers later in life. Her book on fertility and motherhood is:
Manifesting Baby: The Mother's 30 Day Fertility Journal www.manifestingbaby.com
http://inlovewithme.com/life-coaching

Parenting and Divorce Resources

Parent Coaching:
Work one on one with Shannon and learn how to be the best parent and co-parent possible. A true gift to yourself and your children. Use coupon code **lifedeal** to receive a 25% discount on life coaching sessions.
http://inlovewithme.com/life-coaching

Parenting and Divorce Books:
The 7 Fatal Mistakes Divorced and Separated Parents Make: Strategies for Raising Healthy Children of Divorce and Conflict
Shannon's best-selling parenting and divorce book, give your kids this gift. Use coupon code **bookdeal** to receive 50% discount.
http://inlovewithme.com/books
OR
Amazon.com: http://bit.ly/divorceparentbook

Healthy Children of Divorce in 10 Simple Steps: Minimize the Effects of Divorce on Your Children
Shannon's second book on divorce and parenting, this comprehensive workbook provides you 10 simple steps to raise healthy children of divorce.
Amazon: http://bit.ly/10stepsdivorceparentbook

Parenting and Divorce Class on Video:
Shannon teaches her highly acclaimed class on children and divorce to provide you the secrets of raising healthy children of divorce. Discounted 50% to $29.99. Use coupon code **happykid** to receive discount.
http://bit.ly/divclass

SOURCES/REFERENCES

Adams, Marilee G. Ph.D. *Change Your Questions, Change Your Life: 10 Powerful Tools for Life and Work*. 2d edition. San Francisco: Berrett-Koehler Publishers, 2009.

Anderson, Susan. *The Journey from Abandonment to Healing: Turning the End of a Relationship into a New Life*. New York: Berkley Publishing Group, 2000.

Bays, Brandon. *The Journey: A Practical Guide to Healing Your Life and Setting Yourself Free*. New York: Fireside, 2002.

Beattie, Melody. *Codependent No More*. Minnesota: Hazelden Foundation, 1986.

Benedek, E.P. MD. & C.F. Brown, M.Ed. *How to Help Your Child Overcome Your Divorce. A Support Guide for Families*. New York: Newmarket Press, 1998.

Gardner, R.A., MD. *The Parents Book about Divorce*. New York: Bantam Books, 1991.

Hannibal, Mary Ellen. *Good Parenting through Your Divorce: How to Recognize, En-courage, and Respond to Your Child's Feelings and Help Them Get through Your Divorce*. New York: Marlowe & Company, 2002.

Hendrix, H. Ph.D. *Getting the Love You Want: A Guide for Couples*. New York: Holt and Company, 1998, 2008.

Hetherington EM, Cox, M, Cox R. Effects of divorce on parents and children. *In ME Lamb (ed.) Non Traditional Families: Parenting And Child Development*. Hillsdale, NJ: Erlbaum, 1982.

Hetherington EM and Kelly, John. *For Better or For Worse: Divorce Reconsidered*. New York: W.W. Norton and Company, 2002.

Hickey, E., MSW & Dalton, E. JD. *Healing Hearts: Helping Children and Adults Recover from Divorce*. Seattle, WA: Gold Leaf Press, 1997.

Jones-Soderman, J. & Quattrocchi, A. *How to Talk to Your Children about Divorce: Understanding What Your Children May Think, Feel and Need*. Family Mediation Publishing Co.: Scottsdale, AZ. 2006.

Kalter, N. Ph.D. *Growing Up with Divorce: Helping Your Child Avoid Immediate and Later Emotional Problems.* Free Press: New York. 1990.

Kelly, Joan B. *Risk and Resiliency for Children of Separation and Divorce: Current Research and Implications for Practice.* Presentation at Loyola University, Chicago, IL, June 2005.

Lansky, Vicki. *Vicki Lansky's Divorce Book for Parents.* Minnetonka, MN: Book Peddlers, 2003.

Lipton, Bruce H. PhD. *The Biology of Belief: Unleashing the Power of Consciousness, Matter and Miracles.* Carlsbad, CA: Hay House, 2008.

Long, N, PhD. & R. Forehand, Ph.D. *Making Divorce Easier on Your Child: 50 Effective Ways to Help Children Adjust.* Chicago: Contemporary Books, 2002.

Marquardt, E. *Between Two Worlds: The Inner Lives of Children of Divorce.* New York: Three Rivers Press, 2005.

Marston, S. *The Divorced Parent: Success Strategies for Raining Your Children after Separation.* New York: William Morrow and Company, 1994.

Mate, Gabor, MD. *How Attention Deficit Disorder Originates and What You Can Do About It.* New York: Plume, 1999.

McGraw, Phil. Ph.D. *Love Smart: Find the One You Want, Fix the One You Got.* New York: Free Press, 2005.

Neuman, M.G. & P. Romanowski. *Helping Your Kids Cope with Divorce the Sandcastles Way.* New York: Random House, 1998.

Oddenino, Michael L. *Putting Kids First: Walking Away From a Marriage without Walking All Over the Kids.* Family Connections Publishing: USA, 1995.

Ross, J.A, M.A. & J. Corcoran. *Joint Custody with a Jerk: Raising a Child with an Uncooperative Ex.* New York: St. Martin's Press, 1996.

Schneider, M.F. & Zuckerberg, J. Ph.D. *Difficult Questions Kids Ask: And Are Too Afraid to Ask About Divorce.* New York: Fireside, 1996.

Stahl, P.M. Ph.D. *Parenting after Divorce: A Guide to Resolving Conflicts and Meeting Your Children's Needs.* Atascadero, CA: Impact Publishers, 2000.

Thich Nat Hanh. *True Love: A Practice for Awakening the Heart.* Boston: Shambala Publications, 1997.

Thomas, S. Ph.D. *Parents Are Forever: A Step-by-Step Guide to Becoming Successful Co-parents After Divorce.* Longmont, CO: Springboard Publications, 2004.

Thomas, S. Ph.D. *Two Happy Homes: A Working Guide for Parents & Stepparents after Divorce and Remarriage.* Longmont, CO: Springboard Publications, 2005

Wallerstein, J. S. & S. Blakeslee. *What about the Kids? Raising Your Children Before, During and After Divorce.* New York: Hyperion, 2003.

Wallerstein, J.S., J. M. Lewis, & S. Blakeslee. *The Unexpected Legacy of Divorce: A 25-Year Landmark Study.* New York: Hyperion, 2000.

Welwood, John. *Perfect Love: Imperfect Relationships.* Boston: Trumpeter, 2007.

Woodward Thomas, K. *Calling in the One: 7 Weeks to Attract the Love of Your Life.* New York: Three Rivers Press, 2004.

Made in the USA
Las Vegas, NV
20 March 2021